BE BRAVE

An Unlikely Manual for Erasing Heartbreak

J. M. Farkas

Andrews McMeel
PUBLISHING®

Andrews McMeel Publishing
a division of Andrews McMeel Universal
1130 Walnut Street, Kansas City, Missouri 64106

www.andrewsmcmeel.com

18 19 20 21 22 SDB 10 9 8 7 6 5 4 3 2 1

ISBN: 978-1-4494-8976-2

Library of Congress Control Number: 2017955921

Editor: Patty Rice
Art Director: Holly Swayne
Production Editor: David Shaw
Production Manager: Cliff Koehler

Introduction

Sometimes you think you're writing to one person, but it turns out you're writing to someone else.

At first, I thought I wrote *Be Brave* for myself. To myself. Because it was exactly what I needed to hear at the time. It was an act of compassion and consolation. Because I was standing in a used bookstore in Boca Raton, Florida, and pretending that I was just struggling with writer's block. Because someone who had come into and out of and back into my life, had left again and never really came back. Because I missed him. Because I had to somehow find a way to unsplit my own obliterated heart.

And then, I realized, I also wrote this book for my former high school English students. *Be Brave* is a love letter to teaching (and my teachers). To my students who taught me so much and helped me become a writer. I hope they'll remember me and my rebelliousness and my obsession with trying to make literature more relevant to their lives. I hope more than anything that in learning to care about books and reading and sharing their writing, they learned to care more about each other too.

But it turned out that I wrote this book mostly for the person who will never read it: my grandmother, Ma. (You'll meet her in the dedication at the back of this book.)

And now for you. Whoever you are, holding these words or maybe your own broken heart in your open hands—I wrote this book for you too.

*

I believe in a kind of Book-Fate. That certain books, like certain people, come into and out of and back into your life at just the right time and for just the right reason. So there I was in that used bookstore, sliding my fingers down the torn spine of *Beowulf*. It was the Burton Raffel translation. It was the exact same version of the book that I taught to ninth graders during my very first year as a high school English teacher. I remember that I had to reread the pages the night before I would teach them. I was basically doing the exact same homework I had assigned to my students.

You can ask any of my students: I was not the typical English teacher. My atypical background probably had something to do with it. I'm a dental school dropout. My first job out of college was at a dating service. I guess you can say my pedagogy was unconventional too. On a midterm, I had a multiple-choice section that included questions about the students in my class, and the things that they had revealed about themselves or shared during class discussion. I wanted to see if the kids were learning from and paying attention to each other, not just their grades or whatever letter was written on top of their papers in my anything-but-red pen. I was transparent and unapologetic about creating a kind of *Breakfast Club* experience. Through group assignments and carefully crafted pairings, I pushed my students to get to know each other. I was obsessively connecting literature to my students' lives and to each other. I believed and still believe that books and creative writing are amazing conduits for developing empathy and creating true classroom community.

Teaching was the hardest and most meaningful job I ever had. The thing about teaching that most people don't understand is—one of the reasons why it's so intimate, so powerful—you get to witness a kind of growth and beauty that most never see. It's like time-lapse photography. And you're privileged to discover your students and their potential before the whole world does. Also, teenagers are notoriously hilarious and honest and heartbreaking and infuriating and amazing. They call you out and keep you on your toes and force you to be utterly yourself. Working with my students and their writing felt like an incredibly fulfilling and creative act. It almost felt like writing. It felt so much like writing that while I was teaching, I stopped pursuing my own writing altogether.

And perhaps the greatest lesson I ended up offering my students turned out to be: quitting teaching. I let go of the profession that I still consider my calling and went on to pursue an MFA in poetry because I was letting my own dreams slip through my own fingers.

Fast-forward to another bookstore, this time when I was a graduate student in Montpelier, Vermont.

Although I had used Austin Kleon's fantastic *Newspaper Blackout* with my high school students, I remember the exact moment I encountered the erasure of an entire book. I opened up the pages of *Nets* by Jen Bervin, who would also become one of my most influential teachers. She had erased the sonnets of Shakespeare, and I was absolutely blown away. I also studied with another erasurist and poet, Mary Ruefle, who authored *A Little White Shadow*. She let me experiment with my own erasure projects, instead of writing the required critical essays. I was wooed by the rebelliousness of erasure. By the extreme attention to language and the visual drama that absence creates on the page. The act of blacking out text sparks one of the central questions I have for myself as a writer: what can I get away with?

Erasure is feisty and irreverent and more fun than writing because you are essentially not-writing. It's almost the opposite of writing, which is why I often turn to it when I'm struggling with writer's block, or when I just feel like I want to "loosen my tongue." Erasure is also collaborative. You are communing across time and space with the original text and writer, and in my case, with the translator too.

But it's the playfulness of erasure that perhaps most speaks to me. It's like a literary mix of hide-and-seek and word search and show-and-tell. People are surprised to learn that I don't actually read the words of the book I am erasing while I'm erasing it. It's a mysterious process, the way certain words seem to lift up, almost phosphoresce off of the page. Sometimes a sequence of words will light up like a string of little lights in summer.

The creation and construction of *Be Brave* was a particularly physical process. I'm so proud that this is a handmade book. Because I used Sharpies to black out the very thin pages, the ink would bleed to the other side. I had to buy several copies of *Beowulf* on used book sites. I had to tear the pages out of the books. I only had a limited number of tries to get it right because permanent markers are unforgiving and because many of the used books I received were highlighted or had notes from students scribbled into the margins. Interestingly, it was often the last pages of the book that were still left untouched, suggesting that students never quite made it to the end of *Beowulf*.

What I was not expecting to discover—erasure is also about faith. A trust that everything you need, everything you want, the exact word you are searching for, that you're hoping might appear next, is often waiting for you on the very next page. Your job is to be still. To stay there until you find it.

After I erased *Beowulf*, this project expanded in scope and into a series. I realized that the audience of *Be Brave* is explicitly female, and I wanted to run with this idea. It never sat well with me that the canon and the classic high school English syllabus are so expressly male. So I decided that I wanted to continue to pursue erasure with more purpose. I wanted to spin a feminist-revisionist twist on the classics. I wanted to create books for females about females by a female to empower females. *Be Brave* is just the beginning.

BE

brave

5

10

15

20

refuse

his

shining

Be

55

fierce

and

60

swelled

65

and

resolved

70

and young

75

and

over   it

80

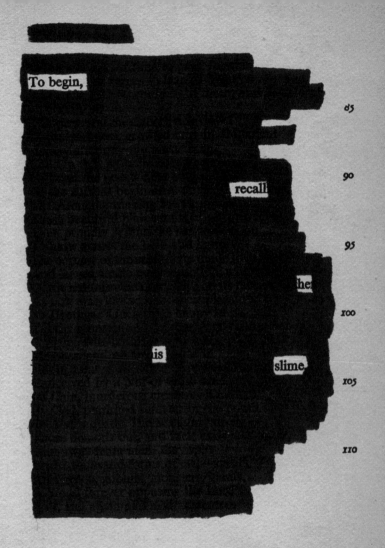

To begin,

recall

the

is

slime.

12

sprawled in

her

knowing   bed

delighted

by

Her

empty

hands.

follow

his

bent.

heart

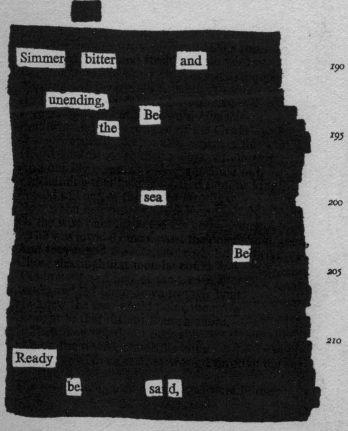

Simmer bitter and

unending,

the Be

the

sea

Be

Ready

be said,

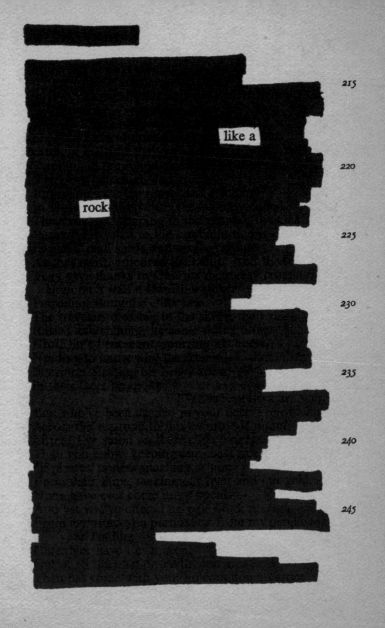

like a

rock

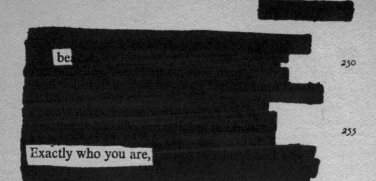

be.

Exactly who you are,

250

255

260

265

270

275

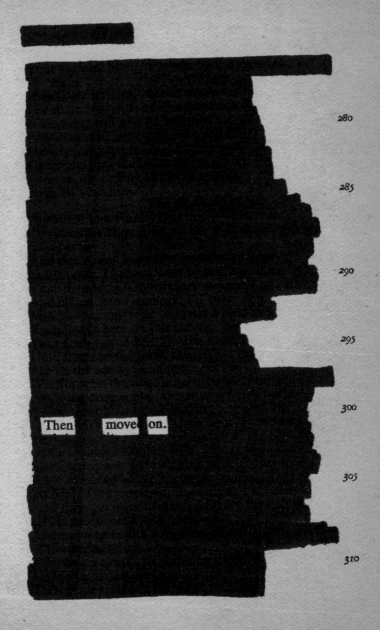

Then move on.

280

285

290

295

300

305

310

18

315

Like a   320

                    song

                                                            325

                                                            330

                                                            335

Be

340

345

350

355

360

alone. 365

370

No

waiting for   promises

under

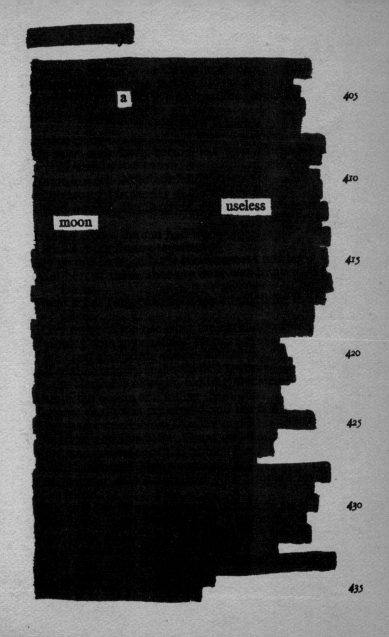

a

useless

moon

405
410
415
420
425
430
435

440

445

450

455

because you were afraid

460

465

470

try to

475

480

485

Be

490

A poet

495

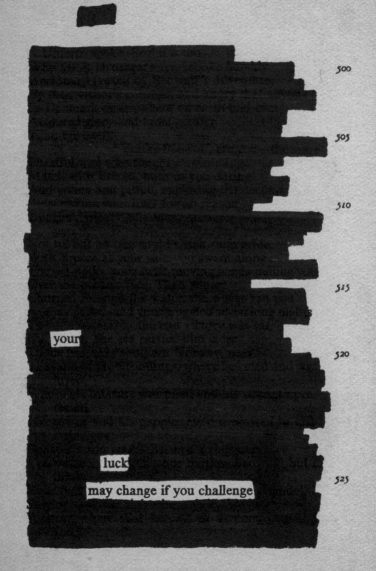

your

luck

may change if you challenge

your tongue

530

535

540

545

550

555

To be true.

560

565

570

575

580

585

590

595

600

605

610

615

620

thank God for

625

630

great

635

music

640

645

650

655

660

sleep and

665

670

675

680

685

690

695

700

Be

705

eager
and angry at the thought of

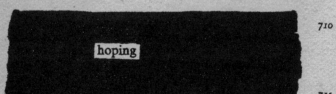

710

hoping

715

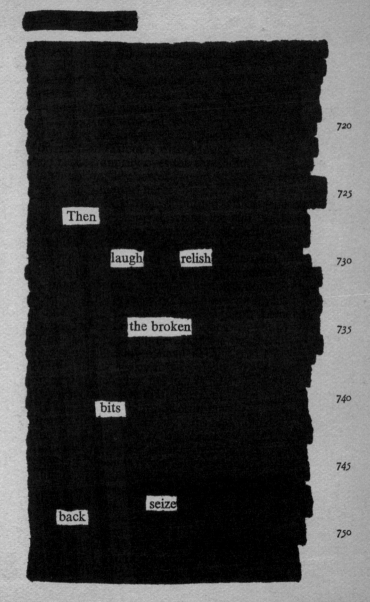

720

725

Then

laugh   relish   730

the broken   735

740

bits

745

seize

back   750

755

760

765

770

the

775

780

star

in

785

the

throat,

33

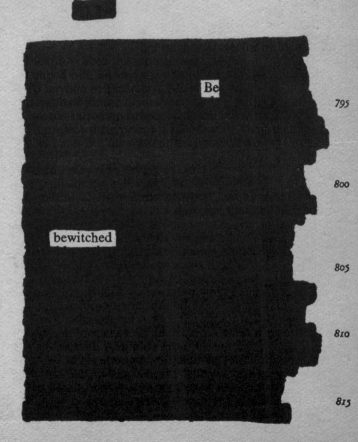

Be

bewitched

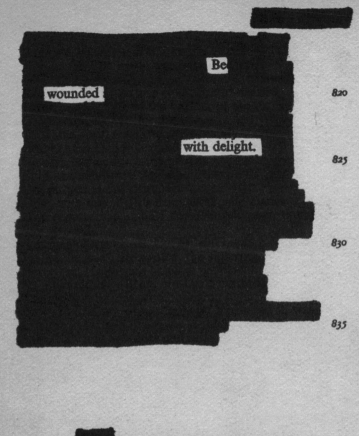

Be

wounded

with delight,

820

825

830

835

840

845

850

855

860

865

And sometimes

sing

870

To

struggle

875

880

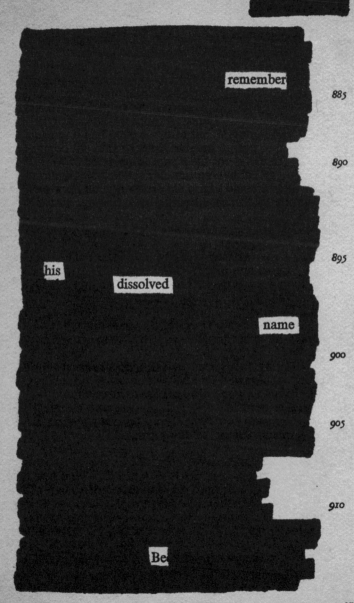

remember

his

dissolved

name

Be

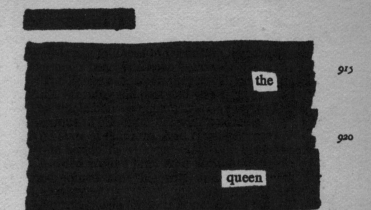

the 915

920

queen

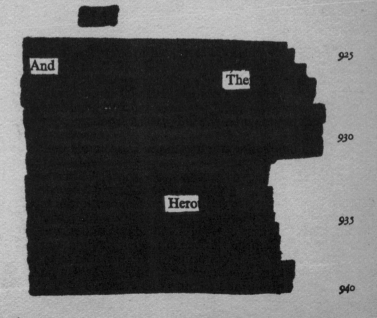

And 925

The

930

Hero

935

940

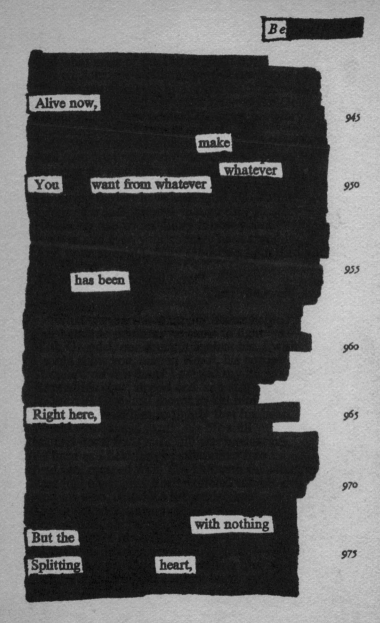

Be

Alive now,

945

make

whatever

You   want from whatever

950

has been

955

960

Right here,

965

970

with nothing

But the

975

Splitting   heart,

From running wildly
no one
Wanting to go,
wherever

990

985

980

995

1000

1005

Be

golden

1010

1015

1020

1025

1030

1035

1040

41

Be

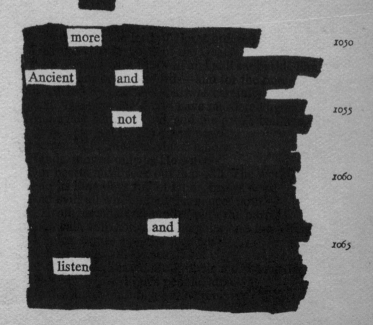

more

1050

Ancient   and

1055

not

and

1065

listen

1070

:.

1075

1080

1085

1090

accept 1095

what

1100

is

1105

43

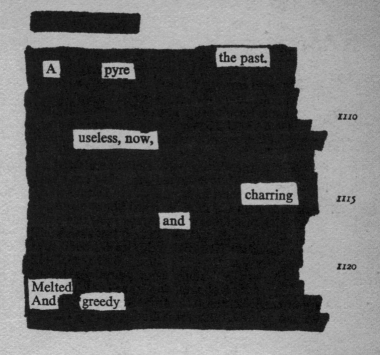

A   pyre   the past.

useless, now,

charring

and

Melted
And   greedy

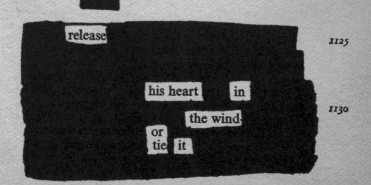

release

his heart   in

the wind

or
tie it

to

1135

1140

1145

1150

her

1155

1160

peacefully

1165

know
you have shown

1170

1175

1180

1185

1190

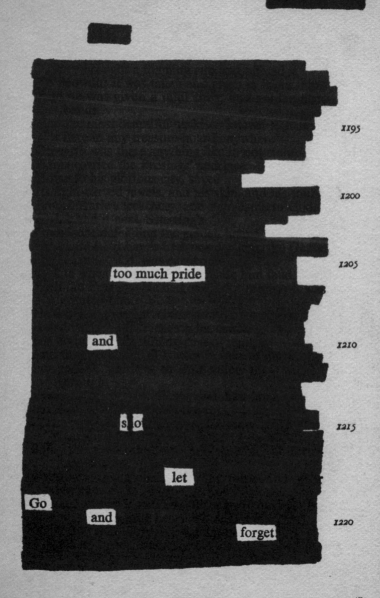

too much pride

and

1195

1200

1205

1210

s o

1215

let

Go

and

forget

1220

47

them

brood on

grace

1255

1260

1265

1270

1275

1280

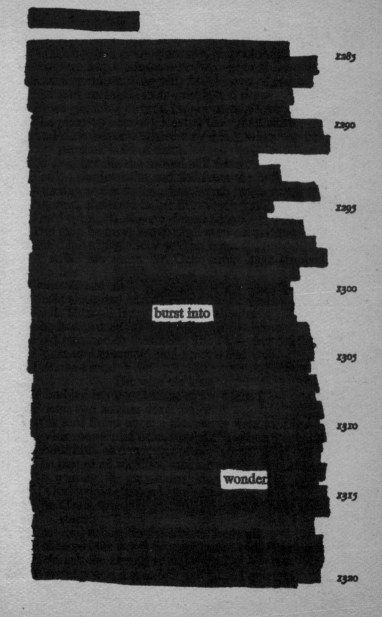

burst into

wonder

1285

1290

1295

1300

1305

1310

1315

1320

you
mighty

female creature.

1325

1330

1335

1340

1345

1350

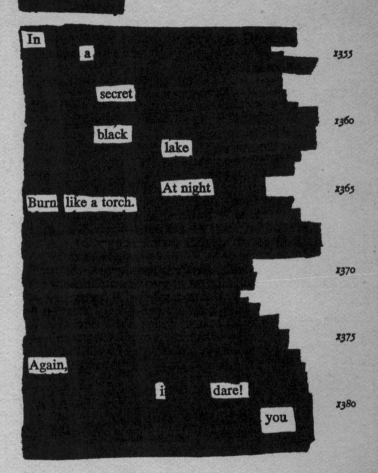

In
    a

       secret

       black
               lake

               At night
Burn like a torch.

Again,

             i   dare!
                  you

1355

1360

1365

1370

1375

1380

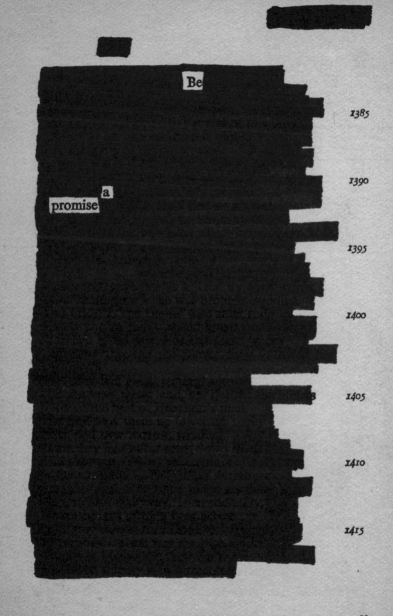

Be

promise a

1385

1390

1395

1400

1405

1410

1415

Be   an arrow

1420

1425

1430

1435

1440

1445

1450

swirling

1455

1460

1465

1470

1475

1480

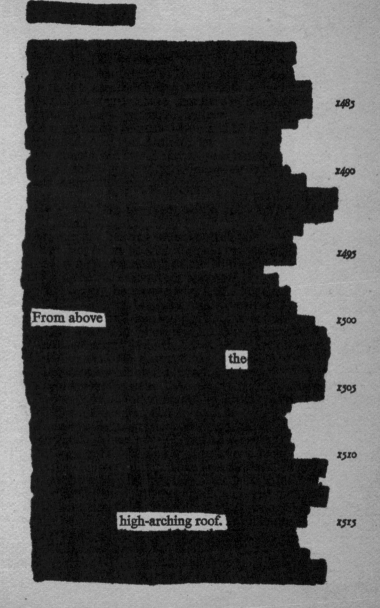

From above

the

high-arching roof.

1485

1490

1495

1500

1505

1510

1515

1520

1525

1530

1535

ready to leap

1540

1545

To

the 1550

bottom of the earth,

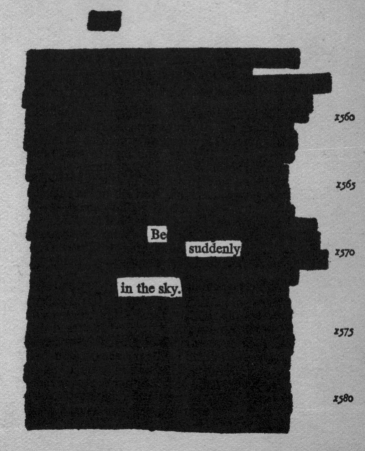

1555

1560

1565

Be   suddenly

in the sky.

1570

1575

1580

Be

the

sun

sadly, watching,

1585

1590

1595

1600

1605

1610

1615

Be

weird

1620

1625

1630

1635

1640

1645

1650

do nothing,

1655

1660

1665

1670

1675

1680

61

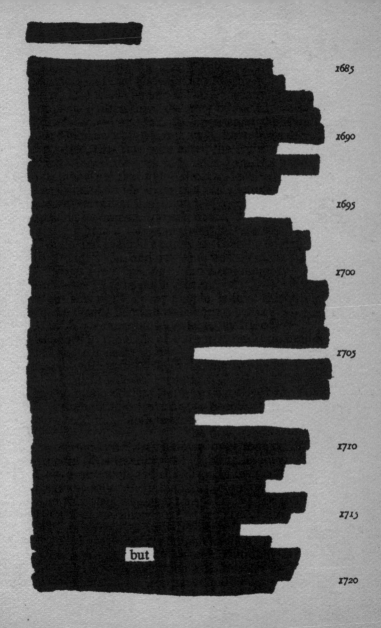

but

1725

1730

1735

flourish

1740

1745

Remember

and forget

1750

1755

1760

1765

1770

1775

1780

Go   go   :   be

morning

1785

1790

1795

1800

and

begin

1805

1810

eager to be

1815

waiting

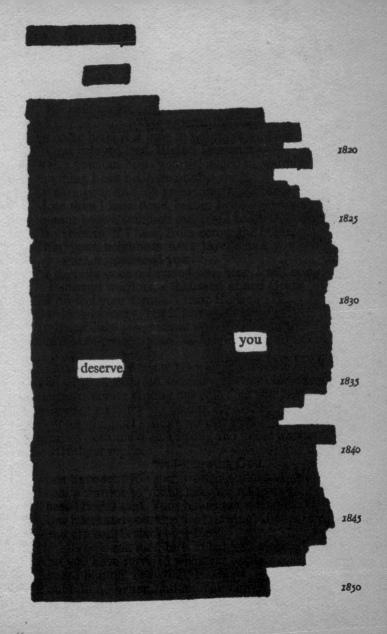

1820

1825

1830

you

deserve

1835

1840

1845

1850

66

love

1855

1860

1865

1870

1875

1880

1885

Too,

1890

1895

1900

1905

1910

1915

1920

1925

1930

And

1935

1940

1945

now,

1950

69

1955

1960

1965

1970

1975

1980

to

your search

1985

1990

1995

2000

2005

2010

2015

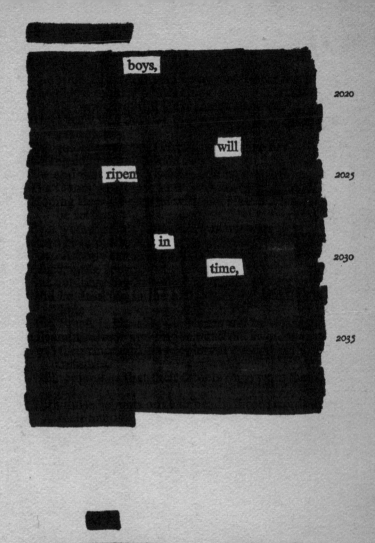

boys,

2020

will

ripen

2025

in

time,

2030

2035

2040

72

2045

2050

2055

2060

2065

to know everything, you need 2070

2075

meant to leave

2080

2085

2090

2095

2100

could not

return

2105

2110

·115

2120

2125

2130

2135

2140

to you,

2145

2150

2155

2160

2165

trust

2170

2175

that

2180

2185

2190

2195

2200

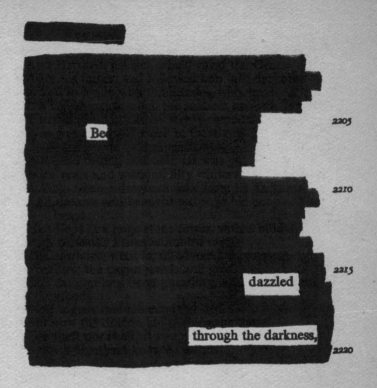

Bee

2205

2210

dazzled

2215

through the darkness,

2220

2225

watch
fate,

lift

On its swift wings,

2265

2270

2275

2280

2285

2290

2295

and

fly

2300

2305

2310

2315

2320

2325

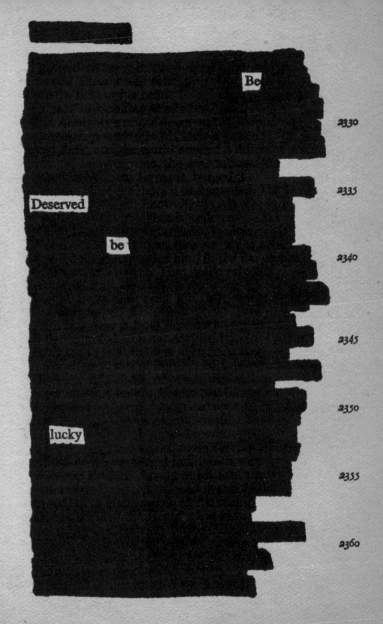

Be

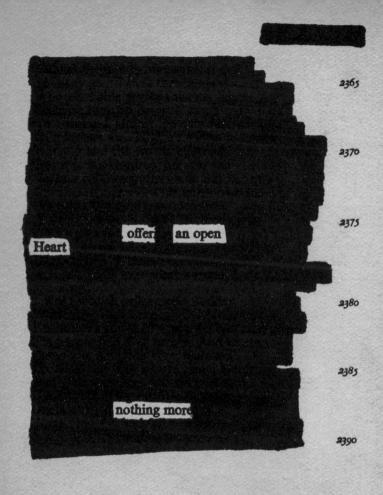

2365

2370

2375

Heart   offer   an open

2380

2385

nothing more

2390

Be

a

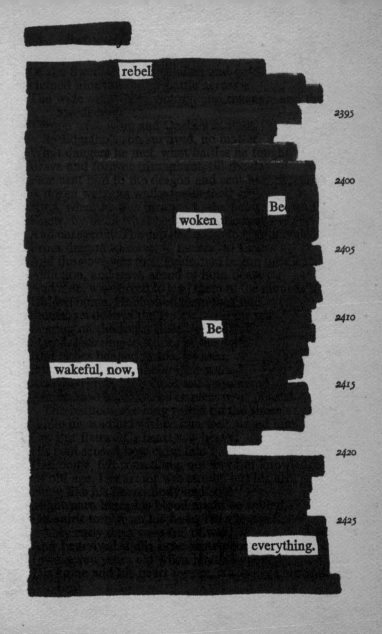

rebel

Be

woken

Be

wakeful, now,

everything.

is possible.

2430

2435

2440

2445

2450

2455

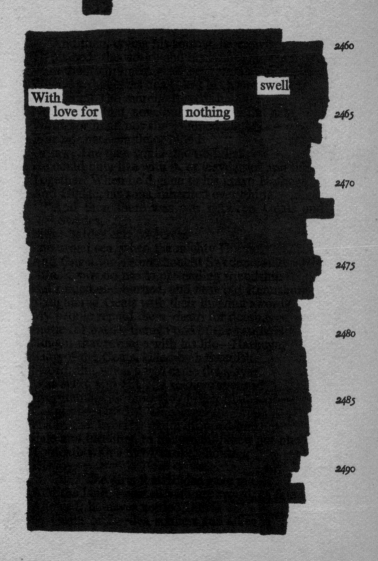

With
love for
nothing
swell

2495

2500

2505

Be

endless

2510

2515

2520

2525

2530

2570

Be

2575

2580

2585

that excellent.

2590

2595

2600

2605

2610

2615

2620

Be

2625

2630

90

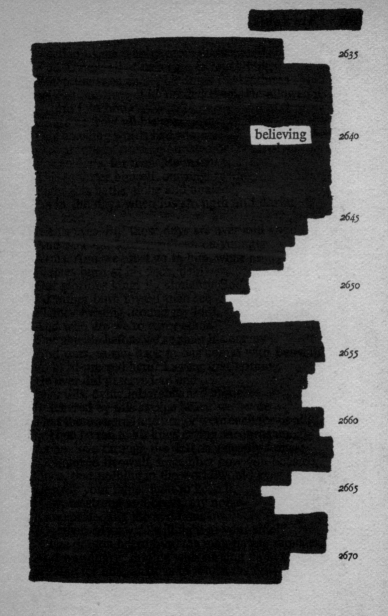

believing

2635

2640

2645

2650

2655

2660

2665

2670

like rain.

Be

loosened

2700

2705

2710

2715

2720

2725

2730

2735

2740

2745

2750

Be

2755

beautifully 2760

Beholding

2805

2810

2815

2820

2825

always and always

2830

2835

2840

2845

2850

2855

2860

better

2895

2900

2905

2910

2915

2920

To   dare too much.

be   lightning

2925

2930

2935

amuse the birds,

2940

2945

2950

2955

across the field,

2960

2965

2970

2975

2980

2985

2990

hurry to
the

bright

truth.

3035

3040

3045

3050

3055

And

destined

3060

3065

3070

3075

3080

Be   worth   3085

it

3090

carry

No

fear

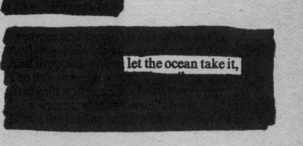

let the ocean take it,

3130

3135

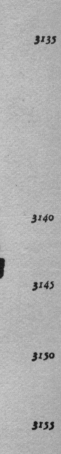

Be

3140

3145

infinite

3150

Be

3155

willing

3160

3165

3170

3175

Be lovèd

3180

Dedication

I submitted *Be Brave* for publication because and when
my grandmother, Ma, passed away. Because death is
life's greatest teacher. Because I was forced to confront
myself and things I wanted in life, but was too afraid to
admit or to pursue. Because I was grieving. Because I was
missing my grandmother, and I was missing the person
Ma made me believe I could be. So in a completely new
context and as an aspiring writer, I wanted and needed
to: be brave.

Perhaps the most meaningful surprise to come out
of this book is that my grandmother somehow found
her way onto its cover. I was cleaning out her apartment
and placing her old clothes into bags to donate to local
charities. Searching through Ma's things, I discovered
the most beautiful photo of my grandmother from when
she was young. Like the unerased words inside this book,
this image was also waiting for me all along. I knew it
was meant to be.

*

The truth is, I never intended for this book to be
anything more than a personal project. And for many,
many months after I finished the blackout, it sat in a
dark drawer. But then I lost one of the most important

people in my life. My grandmother passed away after a grueling year of fighting for her recovery.

And now, I want to tell you about Ma. Not just because she was such a remarkable person, but because this book would have never existed without her.

My grandmother Eva Wohlberg Braun was born on March 13, 1930, in Hajdúszoboszló, a small Hungarian town. The year she was born, the mineral springs burst from the ground and the town became a summer retreat for spa treatments. She had loving parents named Bela and Olga Wohlberg. She had a sister, Agnes, who was a year and a half younger.

Ma was fourteen when she was taken to Auschwitz with her family in a cattle car. She was liberated when she was fifteen and was the only family member to survive the Holocaust. She met her beloved *veszett kutya* husband, Joseph Braun, in 1950 in Budapest, and they had two children. The Hungarian Revolution broke out in 1956, and they escaped across the border hidden under a tarp in a horse-drawn carriage. The Brauns eventually immigrated to the United States to start a new life. Ma loved America. She worked for ten years in a sewing sweatshop making zippers for one dollar a dozen, and then later in her husband's dental lab. All the while, she was extremely present and involved in every aspect of her children and grandchildren's lives.

Ma had the ability to make everyone and anyone feel special. She made the best chicken soup, a.k.a. Ma Soup. She told whichever grandchild she was with that he or she was The Favorite. She was a great listener. She was incredibly optimistic. Ma had an

obsession with hair and would be the first to "critique"
any family member's 'do. She was the most genuinely
humble person. Ma really didn't grasp the concept
of how special she was. She loved music, especially
opera, and taught her family to love music. Ma loved
the Catskills and Florida. She was an incredible
storyteller. Everything was a love story, and all the
people in her life and the things that happened were
"meant to be," down to the stomachache she had
when she met her husband. Ma outlasted everyone on
the dance floor. She was a workout fiend and loved to
compete: fifty laps a day in the pool, eighteen holes of
golf, yoga, bridge, beer pong, bowling (she once rolled
a 184 in her late seventies). She loved to check Twitter
and text, and was an avid emoji user. She had a special
smile. She worried for us. She prayed for us. She loved
chewing on bones. She loved taking baths. Ma made us
feel great and had superhero-like powers to pinch our
cheeks and say the word *cukorka*. Any worries, fears,
doubts, and sorrows melted away with her warmth
and confidence in us. She epitomized selflessness. She
gave up her king bed when we visited her "paradise" in
Boca. She had a million friends and made a new friend
every time she went to the mailbox. Despite completing
only an eighth-grade education, she was brilliant in math
and could multiply triple digits in her head. She loved
sushi and the Knicks and New Year's Eve celebrations
with sparkling cider. She was a genius with people and
navigating relationships. I lovingly referred to Ma as
"The Master Manipulator" because she could convince
you to do anything and somehow also convince you

that you came to that decision on your own. Her trade-mark candy was a Kit Kat. She was grateful. She thought crying was good for you. Ma loved her family fiercely. She was the proudest wife, mother, grandmother, and great-grandmother you could ever imagine.

Family was everything to Ma.

She was everything to her family too.

*

This book is dedicated to my grandmother, who I miss every day. For Ma, who made me believe I was The Favorite—who was the bravest.